D0366684

Wildlife Woodcraft

Lois Brandt Phillips

Naturegraph

Library of Congress Cataloging in Publication Data $\overline{\text{CIP}}$

Phillips, Lois Brandt.
    Wildlife woodcraft.

    SUMMARY: Presents step-by-step instructions for na-
ture craft projects including plaques, boxes, wooden items,
and three-dimensional scenes set in logs.
    1. Nature craft. 2. Design, Decorative—Animal forms.
[1. Nature craft. 2. Handicraft] I. Title.
TT157.P47   745.5   78-5267

Dedication

In memory of my husband and of my son

Copyright © 1978 by Lois Brandt Phillips

ISBN 0-87961-067-0 Cloth Edition
ISBN 0-87961-066-2 Paper Edition

Naturegraph Publishers, Inc., Happy Camp, California 96039

CONTENTS

INTRODUCTION

The crafts in this book came about as an expression of many joyful encounters with nature. A walk along a mountain stream where fern fronds and smooth pebbles were gathered, a picnic in a national park where golden-mantled squirrels boldly begged for crumbs, hours spent watching the antics of raccoons both outdoors and from my window.

With wildlife art, the beauty of the forest can be brought into your home and put into lasting form for future enjoyment. Life-size animals peeking from "hollow logs" are a handsome addition to any room of the house. Using nature's designs with three-dimensional crafting, you can decorate unusual plaques, boxes and wooden items. These items are fun to make and give as gifts, and this book will help you to get started in creating your own souvenirs of nature.

As with all worthwhile projects, time and patience are required, as well as a love for the creatures of the woods. Materials are minimal and readily available; many can be found on your outdoor excursions. Begin by collecting lumber scraps, interesting shapes of weathered wood, and smooth stones. Press ferns, grasses and various other plants between layers of newspaper so they will dry and be ready to use.

It helps to keep a file of wildlife photos and magazine clippings for reference. Keen observation of animals and birds is important. Nature books from your local library, museum displays of animals and birds, and taxidermists can all be of help in supplying pictures and models for realistic rendering in your artwork.

All projects in this book were painted with acrylic paints.

These paints can be applied directly to sanded wood or onto stones with no previous treatment of the surfaces. They dry within a few minutes so projects can be completed quickly. Remember always to keep a jar of water handy in which to rest your brushes, for acrylic paint dried on brushes is difficult to remove.

Read through the directions to each project carefully. Thoroughly plan your design before touching brush to board. Then proceed through each step until completion. Do not get discouraged; often it is only in the final steps that the project attractively emerges. Your reward will be a charming woodland piece you or your friends can enjoy for many years to come.

Chapter One

LOG CREATURES

The hollow tree stump, the rotted tree, the decayed log lying on the forest floor: all are purposeful in nature and each is uniquely beautiful. Raccoons use the hollow tree as a den, raising generation after generation of young, as long as the tree stands. Gray squirrels may evict a family of owls from their nest hole in a tree and set up housekeeping. Hollow logs are often occupied by different kinds of wildlife in the forest, such as: a rabbit—seeking escape from a predator; chipmunks—frolicing in one end and out the other for the fun of it; a bear—seeking a snug home to hibernate during the winter.

The designs that follow may stir your imagination. You will undoubtably think of other creatures that will for some reason, occupy a hollow log. Try, also, arranging the animals in different positions—rest a head on paws, close eyes assimilating sleep.

HOW TO MAKE LOGS

Since it is difficult to obtain a round slice of log that does not split in wide cracks through the center and whose bark does not flake off, it is best to make your own log-slice.

From a lumber company purchase a 3-inch thick by 16-inch wide board (if board is rough-cut, have it planed), and have it cut into 16-inch blocks. You may get 8 or 9 blocks from a board. Draw a pattern from which to cut log rounds from these blocks (*Fig. 1*). A slightly irregular oval pattern is easy to design. Because of the thickness of the wood, it will be necessary to have the blocks cut by bandsaw. Usually the lumber company will do this for you if you provide the pattern. If the wood is unseasoned, allow the rounds to dry for several weeks in an arid place. They may crack somewhat, but these cracks will not be so deep as to detract from your design. In fact they may be used as part of the design; you might even wish to paint in more fake cracks. Sand front-side smooth. The backside may be sanded just enough to remove slivers.

Figure 1. Cut slightly irregular round from wood block.

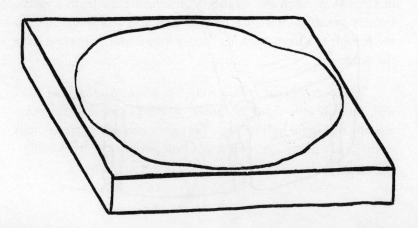

Using a carving tool with a wide curved blade, chisel out grooves about four inches apart all around the sides of the board (*Fig. 2*). This grooving may also be done by using an electric drill with a stone attachment. With your tool or with coarse sandpaper, go around top edge of board to slightly bevel. Sand lightly with medium sandpaper over all carving to remove rough pieces of wood.

On front surface of board about ½-inch from the edge, carve a wavering line around to represent the inner thickness of bark.

MOLDING AND PAINTING BARK

To simulate rough fir bark, apply wood putty between (not in) grooves. Spread putty thinly using circular movements with the knife (*Fig. 3*). Allow it to dry thoroughly. Before painting, lightly brush the sides with your hand to remove loose pieces of putty.

Figure 2. Chisel out grooves about 4 inches apart.

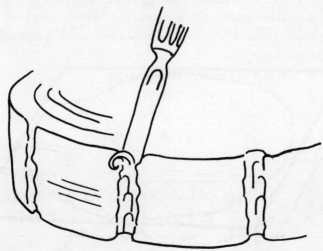

Work on a newspaper-covered surface while painting. A lazy-susan turntable is handy for moving the wood around as you paint. Acrylic colors used for bark are black, red oxide, and burnt umber.

Using black thinned with one part water, paint in all grooves (*Photo 1*). Remember this is to be bark. No carefully drawn lines are required; rather, use a loose dabbing style of painting, but do apply the paint solidly with no spots of unpainted wood showing beneath.

Now mix red oxide in two puddles: one of a watery consistency; the other thick, using very little water. The watery paint will be used to slightly stain areas about an inch or two in width between two black grooves. This will be the highlighted areas of the bark. Gradually darken with thick red oxide, then burnt umber as you near the black grooves.

When all the board's side surface has been covered, use a small brush dipped in black paint and make spots and jagged lines here and there to suggest peeling bark (*Photo 2*). With the same three colors paint the ½-inch band of bark along the top surface of the board. Now the log is ready for designing (*Photo 3*).

Figure 3. Spread putty in circular movements.

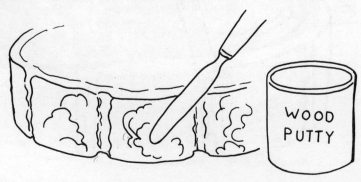

Photo 1. Sides of board have been textured with wood putty; grooves are carved and painted black.

Photo 2. Simulated bark.

Photo 3. Board is ready for design.

Rule one-inch squares on a large sheet of tracing paper. Place the log round on the paper and draw an outline. Using the pattern charts at the end of this book (pp. 57-64) copy one of the designs by enlarging it onto the ruled paper. Trace your enlarged design onto the board with carbon paper.

LOG INHABITANTS

THE VARYING HARE, also called the snowshoe rabbit, is shown here in its brown summer coat (*Photo 4*). It could also be painted in its camouflaged white winter suit. A larger rabbit than the cottontail, it is found in northern states and Canada. Though its preferred home is a simple spot hidden in a thicket, the hare will take cover in a hollow log.

Acrylic colors used in painting the varying hare are black, white, burnt sienna, raw umber, and yellow ochre.

Photo 4. Varying Hare.

Paint the background first. Brush on burnt sienna in curved strokes around the hare to suggest the curve of the hollow log. Dry. Paint black over, allowing some streaks of burnt sienna to show through. Bring black of background right up to the form of the animal, breaking off into jagged lines to suggest fur.

The animal's eyes are the center of interest in your design. Paint them next. Burnt sienna is used around the black pupil; then a highlight of white.

With water-thinned mixtures of burnt sienna and yellow ochre, stain rabbit-shape in graduated shades from light to dark (darkest around hare's back). I find it easiest to control and blend the paint by wrapping several thicknesses of paper towel around my forefinger, dipping it into the paint, and then brushing lightly over the areas to be stained.

Next dip a small sable brush into a thick mixture of black and raw umber. With quick strokes cover hare with fine lines, always painting in the direction of the fur growth. Work rapidly; these lines need not be tediously drawn.

Apply white paint to areas around eyes, ears, face, and under chin. Now with black paint and a very fine brush carefully place whiskers projecting from area around nose.

Using towel-wrapped finger, dip in water-thinned burnt sienna and stain around edge of bark; also around edge of hole and wherever a "crack" is painted.

A thin white mixture brushed on inside rim will suggest a highlight.

When dry, give the entire front and sides a coat of matte polymer medium. This will be milky white when applied, but drys clear.

Attach two medium-sized screws and picture wire to the back, and now your plaque is ready for hanging.

RACCOONS manage to look mischievious while inno-cently peering from their den in a tree hollow. Many country dwellers have been victims of raccoons' garden or garbage can raids; yet, they are appealing and easily tamed. These small nocturnal carnivores are found in almost every state in America.

Photo 5. Raccoons.

Colors used in this painting (*Photo 5*) are black, white, raw umber and burnt sienna.

As in the directions for the varying hare, paint the background first; then the black eyes, paying particular attention to the highlights that give the bright, alert appearance. Paint the nose black, highlighting it with white.

With thinned raw umber and medium-sized sable brush, paint all dark areas of the raccoon: mask, inner ears, the shadow under the chin. Using a pointed sable brush and raw umber, quickly stroke in lines over head and body to indicate fur. Repeat this procedure, using black paint. Next paint black over mask area and ears, allowing the undercoat of raw umber to show through. Paint white over the eyes, and around ears and nose. With a very fine brush paint white whiskers.

As in previous directions, finish edges with burnt sienna stain. Varnish with matte polymer medium.

GRAY SQUIRRELS play elusively about their tree-top homes in the deep forest. However, they readily tame to city parks and will approach bird feeders or wherever nuts and seeds are scattered.

The gray squirrel shown here (*Photo 6*) is of a western variety. Its tail is a magnificent plume and it is silver-gray in color. The pattern (see p. 59) is basically the same for eastern squirrels, except that the tail should be made slightly smaller and a rusty tone (burnt sienna) added to the face, muzzle, ear, and upper parts of paws.

Follow varying hare directions for background. A light stain of yellow ochre was used first to shade the squirrel. A

Photo 6. Gray Squirrel.

pink tone of burnt umber and white gives the delicate color
to the inside ear. For the salt-and-pepper-colored fur, make
quick strokes of white, then black, using a fine brush. Payne's
gray and white add a silver-gray tone. The squirrel's eye is
raw umber around a black pupil. Outline the tail with white
to give the airy, plumed effect.

THE SCREECH OWL'S name is a misnomer. Its cry is
not a screech; it is a soft, plaintive wail. In a tree cavity the
parents raise about four fuzzy youngsters whose plumage
gradually changes to an irregular pattern (*Photo 7*). In adult-
hood gray or red color phases are common and all have tufts
of feathers resembling ears. It is the best known and most

Photo 7. Screech Owls.

abundant of the owls in North America.

The bright, colorful eyes are the center of interest and are painted first after completing the burnt sienna and black background (see directions under varying hare). Around the large black pupil is a rim of cadmium yellow medium, lightened with white on the lower part, darkened with yellow ochre on the upper rim.

With forefinger wrapped in paper towel, dip in thin mixture of yellow ochre and stain the undercoat of the bird, shading from light to dark around the bird's outer edge.

Using a medium flat sable brush dipped in black acrylic, make short strokes to suggest the barred effect. Be sure to follow the contours of the feathered arrangement around the eyes and across the breast.

To give a fuzzy appearance use white paint with little or no water. Dip brush in paint, wipe off excess and lightly dry-brush each stroke. A thin mixture of raw umber is used to stain in shadows under the wings, beaks, the shady sides of the birds, and the shadow cast by placing one bird slightly in front of the other.

THE COUGAR KITTEN (*Photo 8*) is spotted and has a ringed tail. These markings will fade at about two months of age and it will grow into a tawny adult that is among the largest cats in North America. Like all members of the cat family, the kitten's eyes are a milky blue, changing to golden yellow as it matures. The cougar is also known as puma and mountain lion.

The colors used are yellow ochre, raw sienna, burnt umber, black, and white. After painting iris yellow ochre and raw umber, a stain of cobalt blue is brushed over lightly to give the milky appearance.

Carefully place the typical black patches over the eyes and around the muzzle of the kitten. Other black spots can be placed at random, but be careful to follow the direction of hair growth.

Photo 8. Cougar Kitten.

RED FOX'S intelligent eyes, inquisitive pointed ears and sharp nose, combine to make it the keenest of hunters. Weary from a night of stalking rabbits and mice, this fox (*Photo 9*) has sought concealment in the hollow log to lie and doze until hunger drives it to hunt again.

Photo 9. Red Fox.

Background is painted first, following directions under varying hare. Colors used in painting the fox are yellow ochre, cadmium yellow, burnt sienna, black, and white.

Take time to work the golden lights into the colorful iris. Use cadmium yellow with a touch of burnt sienna for this. The black pupil is slightly elliptical in shape.

Make a stain of burnt sienna and yellow ochre, use paper-towel-wrapped finger to shade the head and body of the fox. Paint black nose and lines around nose and eyes, and darkest shadows of inner ears.

Legs of fox have an undercoat of burnt sienna over which black fur is painted.

Raw umber shades inner ears, under chin and between paws. Accent with white as shown. Varnish with matte polymer medium.

BEAR CUB has found a hollow log in which to play. You can be sure its mother is close by, for she will watch over it until the cub is approximately two years old. A hollow log may serve as a snug home in which it will hibernate during the winter months.

The cub (*Photo 10*) is painted in raw umber and black. An undercoat of burnt sienna is first painted in the shadowed areas—around eyes, under chin, top of head, and inner ears.

A flat sable brush seems to work the best for painting in the many lines required for the fur. Dip brush in paint, remove excess on a piece of newspaper, and use edge of bristles to make fine lines.

Do not make the cub's eye pupils a distinct black. Give them a cloudy appearance by brushing over and around black pupils with raw umber. Remember to put in shadows (raw umber and burnt sienna) next to the bear's paws. Finish with a varnish of matte polymer medium.

Photo 10. Bear Cub.

THE GOLDEN-MANTLED SQUIRREL is a scene stealer in our western national parks where it scampers up to visitors for handouts of crumbs or peanuts. Its brightly colored coat is marked much like a chipmunk's; but it does not have the black stripe over the eyes as does the chipmunk, and it is larger in size.

Photo 11. Golden-mantled Squirrels.

These animals (*Photo 11*) were painted on a natural slice of log. The board was sanded, design traced on, and the black hole painted around the squirrels. Some white highlights around the hole were added.

Yellow ochre is the predominant color of the golden-mantled squirrel and its rusty colored mantle is painted with burnt sienna. Its shiny eyes are black, highlighted with white. White is used to outline the black stripe on its side and around its black tail. With a thin stain of raw umber, in the foreground, dab in a shadow under the body of the squirrel. Use white to highlight the ears and top of the head. Varnish with matte polymer medium.

RUFFED GROUSE.   After twenty-four days of patient brooding, the grouse chicks have hatched (*Photo 12*). Now the hen and rooster grouse will be busy teaching their young to find insects and seeds in the brushy woodland that they inhabit.   The markings on the chicks make them almost invisible among the plants where they hide from danger.

Colors used are burnt sienna, yellow ochre, cadmium yellow medium, white, and black.

After painting the background with burnt sienna and black, use these same two colors for the hen grouse's eye.

With yellow ochre, mark in feather contours over the entire body; smallest across the breast, larger on the back, and largest on the wing. Accent feathers with burnt sienna and black. Paint in white as shown, stroking in direction of feather growth.

The chick's feathers are done in yellow ochre mixed with cadmium yellow medium.   The crowns of their heads are burnt sienna accented with black.

Nest grasses are cadmium yellow medium, yellow ochre, and black.

Varnish with matte polymer medium.

Photo 12. Ruffed Grouse.

MINI LOG PLAQUES

Miniature plaques are made using the same methods as large plaques. Cut 1-inch slices of tree branches of various size in diameter or cut out small rounds from a board, simulating tree bark as with large plaques.

In keeping with the scaled down size, smaller animals such as mice and chipmunks are painted peeking from the holes. Finish with matte polymer medium.

The miniature plaques can be hung singly or can be mounted in shadow box frames. Also attractive is an arrangement of several mini plaques on a strip of burlap. Cut out a narrow strip of burlap in a complimentary color. Machine stitch a 1-inch border on two sides and fringe by pulling threads to ¾-inch all around. Hem the two ends. Glue on plaques. Sew ring to top of burlap strip to hang.

The small plaques shown (*Photo 13*) are grouped on a larger board that has been painted first and to which a decorative hanger ring has been attached at the top.

Photo 13. Mini Plaques.

Chapter Two

3-D CRAFTING

3-D crafting is an easy way to achieve a woodcarved look. It can be applied to any wood surface, from boxes to various sizes of wood plaques. Suggested materials are: wood cigar boxes, wood canisters, cutting boards, wood coasters, door or cupboard panels, plaques cut from lumber scraps, driftwood, etc. The finished product is amazingly similar to a hand carved piece though little skill is required.

BUNNY BUCKET

Since the cottontail rabbit is particularly fond of clover, I have surrounded it with real, dried clover and ferns. Press plants a week before using.

The materials needed to make a bunny bucket are: a wood bucket (or other wood object large enough for the design), acrylic paints (most brands work equally as well for these crafts), brushes, polymer medium gloss, tracing paper, carbon paper, Elmer's glue, scissors, gesso, dried plants and heavy cardboard. The cardboard may be egg carton tops, which are easy to cut. Use bumpy surface for top of design. Any carton cardboard of equal thickness, or illustration board, may be used as well.

Directions:

Draw the pattern on heavy cardboard (*Fig. 4*) and cut it out. Manicure scissors are handy in cutting curves or small pieces. Glue eye and outer ear to rabbit. Arrange rabbit cutout, tucking ¼ of rabbit's feet and tail under body, with dried clover leaves and ferns in a pleasing pattern on the bucket and lid (*Photo 14*). Glue all pieces in place. It may be necessary to press cardboard pieces down with hands or weighted object until pieces adhere to the wood. Let dry several hours or overnight.

With medium size brush apply gesso thickly over entire design on top of lid and middle strip of bucket. Do *not* apply gesso on rim of bucket or rim of lid (or box rim) as the lid will not fit properly if built up with gesso.

Figure 4. Enlarge pattern for size of Bunny Bucket. Cut out rabbit and parts on solid lines. Dotted lines show placement of parts.

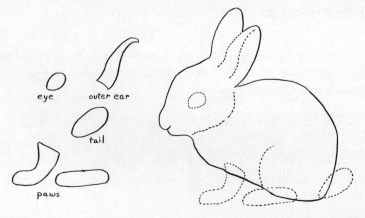

eye   outer ear

tail

paws

Using a small brush, load with gesso and go over design, bearing down on brush so that ridges of gesso delineate rabbit's head and hind legs. Also add vertical ridges of gesso all around bucket. These will stand out in relief and add pleasing texture when bucket is painted and antiqued. Brush gesso thinly over clover so leaf shapes show through (*Photo 15*). Dry thoroughly.

To paint: thin acrylics with water. For the rabbit, mix a small amount of burnt umber with white. Paint this tan mixture over entire rabbit except white areas around eye, ears, stomach and tail. Highlight hind leg and feet with white. The eye is burnt umber around the black pupil.

Make yellow-green by mixing thalo blue and cadmium yellow medium. Paint entire background with this, clover leaves, ferns and all ungessoed wood, inside and out. Highlight leaves and ferns with yellow. Brush white over clover blossoms (*Photo 16*).

When dry, coat evenly over entire outside painted surface with polymer gloss medium. This is milky white and will dry clear. You must apply this protective coat over paint or antique paint will not be removable. Allow several hours or overnight for the gloss varnish to dry.

To antique your design you may use burnt umber or a mixture of burnt umber and black, depending upon how dark you wish the finished product to be. Mix enough water with the paint to make a thin creamy mixture. Apply a section at a time to both the lid and bucket. Allow it to dry a few minutes; then with paper towel or small cloth wrapped around forefinger begin to lightly wipe antiquing away, allowing the paint to remain in crevices and around

Photo 14.　Cardboard cutouts and pressed plants are arranged in a design.

Photo 15.　Apply gesso thickly over rabbit, thinly over clover leaves.

Photo 16. After painting with acrylics, bucket is ready for a coat of gloss polymer medium.

form of rabbit and leaves. If the antique paint dries on design, dampen the cloth with water to remove paint. Allow antiquing to "shade" rabbit by leaving heaviest in shadows of ears, neck, and hind leg. Remove most of antiquing from clover leaves and fern, keeping background darker (*Photo 17*).

You may give a protective coat of varnish to the bucket by painting with gloss or matte polymer medium.

Photo 17. Antiquing is final step to finish Bunny Bucket.

CALIFORNIA QUAIL

The California quail picture is a more ambitious project than the bunny bucket. It is shown here (*Photo 21*) on a wood door panel with inner measurements of 14½" by 18". The same size plywood or pressed wood (masonite) could be used equally as well, framed or unframed.

California quail are common birds in many western states. However, if bobwhite quail is more familiar to you, the same general pattern can be used, omitting the feathered plume on top the head and painting in the characteristic markings of the bobwhite.

Pattern the background with dried foliage which has been pressed between newspaper at least a week. Ferns, grasses, and various leaves may be used.

Figure 5. California Quail on perch. Enlarge pattern. Cut out bird and parts on solid lines. Dotted lines show placement of parts.

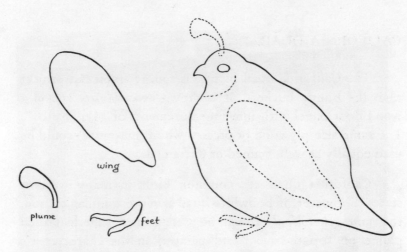

Figure 6. California Quail on ground. Enlarge pattern. Cut out bird
and parts on solid lines. Dotted lines show placement of parts.

Other materials are the same as used for the bucket,
substituting wood panel or board. Acrylic colors used in this
picture are cadmium yellow medium, thalo blue, Payne's gray,
burnt umber, burnt sienna, medium orange, and white.

Draw pattern of quail (*Fig. 5 & 6*) on tracing paper.
Transfer to heavy cardboard with carbon paper and cut out.
From cardboard cut tree branch for the quail to perch on.

Glue wings to quail, arrange birds, branch, dried ferns
and leaves on the board (*Photo 18*). Mark each piece's position with a pencil. Remove and glue on, gluing background
of foliage first, then branch and birds, tucking ¼-inch of
plume and foot under body pieces. Using hands or a weight,
press on large pieces. Let dry several hours or overnight
before applying gesso.

Apply gesso thickly over the entire board. Indicate
feathers on the birds by making ridges with a brush loaded
with gesso. Scalloped lines are made across the breast, small

Photo 18. Cardboard cutouts of California Quail and pressed ferns are glued in place.

feathers on the back and longer ones on the wings. Make ridges on the tree branch also (*Photo 19*).

Paint with cadmium yellow medium thinned with water. Start at the top of the board and gradually shade to bottom with green by adding a bit of thalo blue. Paint entire back-

Photo 19. Board is painted and textured with gesso.

ground, ferns and grasses, but omit birds and branch. Highlight some of the fern tips and leaves with yellow and cadmium orange.   Paint the branch white and burnt umber.
Using the illustration of quail, paint in characteristic markings.   Solid Payne's gray is used on head, plume, mask, and
shoulder markings of birds. Back and wings are thin mixtures

of Payne's gray and umber. Sides are burnt sienna shading to white on breast. Feet are burnt umber marked with Payne's gray.

Coat entire board with gloss polymer medium. Dry several hours or overnight (*Photo 20*).

Photo 20. The painted design is given a coat of gloss polymer medium.

Antique by painting over the design with a thin mixture of burnt umber or burnt umber and black. Allow to dry a few minutes. Remove by brushing lightly with paper towel or cloth, leaving antique paint in crevices and around the birds and ferns. Allow antiquing to remain heaviest in the corners of the picture. Varnish is not necessary.

Photo 21. Antiquing completes picture of California Quail.

WILDFLOWER PLAQUE

Your favorite flower can be the theme of a plaque with a handcarved look. Shown here are brown-eyed Susans (*Photo 22*).

Materials required: 5½" by 15" board, egg carton tops or heavy cardboard, Elmer's glue, gesso, acrylic paint and brushes, polymer medium gloss.

Draw a flower design and cut it out from heavy cardboard. Cut stems to fit the size of your board. Glue in place on the board, stems first, tucking ¼-inch under flowers. Let flowers overlap some stems. Glue centers to the flowers. Dry thoroughly.

Apply a coat of gesso, pressing down with brush to make ridges on flowers to simulate separate petals. Add texture to the background by applying ridges of gesso. Dry overnight.

Paint with water-thinned acrylics. Colors on brown-eyed Susan plaque are: cadmium yellow dark, with touches of cadmium orange on flowers. Background is yellow green— a mixture of cadmium yellow and thalo blue; stems are dark green, made by adding more blue. Centers of flowers are burnt umber. When dry, cover entire surface with polymer medium gloss. Allow to dry 3 or 4 hours.

Antique with water-thinned mixture of burnt umber and black. Dry a few minutes. Gently wipe away surface paint, allowing some to remain in crevices and in the four corners of the plaque. Do not allow antique paint to remain on plaque for longer than a few hours before removing, as it may become difficult to remove. A bit of soap added to a dampened cloth will aid in removing the excess paint.

Photo 22. Brown-eyed Susans.

Chapter Three

WILDLIFE SCENES WITH FIGURINES

FOUR SEASONS

This project uses the interesting bits of wood, moss, rocks, etc., that you have collected. Wooden cigar boxes or small wooden crates contain the scenes.

When planning your scene keep in mind a theme such as the seashore, a mountain stream, or desert. If the seashore is an effect you would like, you might want to try tying bits of driftwood together with cord. This makes a piling on which to glue a seagull figurine. Paint the background blue and glue sand to the bottom of the box to complete the scene.

The color of the background helps determine the effect you create. Colors suggested for the four seasons are as follows: blue and white for winter, yellow and brown for autumn, and shades of green for spring and summer.

If you wish to hang your box, it is best to glue or nail a hanger to the box before you arrange the scene.

SPRING

This scene was kept tiny to make the figurine of the fawn the center of interest. The ground is molded with instant paper mâché (mix with water following directions on package). Press figurine in clay to mark its position, then remove. Paint the inside of the box yellow-green (cadmium yellow medium and thalo blue). Glue a small dried fern to the background. After this, paint the green mixture right over the wet clay mâché. Allow for the painted surface to dry a few minutes and then push the small, dried flowers in place. Dry overnight. Paint outside of the box. Glue fawn in place.

Photo 23. Spring Season.

SUMMER

Beavers are at work cutting aspen trees. The tree is a twig chiseled with a carving tool (save the shavings) and touched up with white and black paint to resemble aspen bark. Paint the outside of the box green by mixing thalo blue and cadmium yellow medium as before.

A simple background was painted directly on the inside of the box with no preparation of wood. Green paint indicates the ground. Green florist's clay was patted around the edge, and dried star flowers poked into it. The tree was glued in place with Elmer's glue, and shavings were glued around the base of tree and stump. The figurines can either be glued or stuck in place with a bit of florist's clay.

Photo 24. Summer Season.

AUTUMN

Fasten hanger to back of box. Glue ferns on background. Mix instant paper mâché to clay consistency. Pat on inside bottom for ground, building higher toward back. Press bits of wood and figures in clay to mark positions, then remove. Make puddle of glue in foreground and sprinkle on sand and small pebbles. Set aside 24 hours to dry. Coat only the background with gesso. Dry. Paint background with cadmium yellow medium shaded to cadmium yellow deep. Paint both ungessoed ground and outside of box raw sienna.

When dry, coat inside with gloss polymer medium. Dry thoroughly. Antique by painting with thin mixture of raw umber and raw sienna. With paper towel or small cloth lightly remove antiquing mixture from ferns and from some of the background. If figurines are not detailed enough to suit you, touch them up with acrylic paint. Glue bits of wood, moss, and figurines in place.

Photo 25. Autumn Season.

WINTER

Fasten hanger to back of box. Glue ferns to background. Build up ground with instant paper mâché mixed to a clay consistency. Press logs and animals to mark position. Press in twigs to prepare a hole. Remove. Dry 24 hours. Gesso background and the paper mâché ground. Dry. Coat entire inside with gloss polymer medium.

Antique background with a thin mixture of thalo blue and water. Wipe off antiquing so that the ferns stand out white against the blue background. Lightly rub a little blue over white ground to suggest shadows on the snow. Sides and back of box were painted thalo blue, made dark by adding very little water to the paint.

Spray artificial snow on log and tree branches or paint top surface with white acrylic or with gesso. When dry, glue log in position marked on ground. Glue figurines or fasten them down with bits of florist's clay (*see Photo 26*).

Photo 26. Winter Season.

Chapter Four

WOODGRAIN NATURE ART

Study the rhythmic patterns on a piece of fir plywood or other type of board. With a little imagination you may see the course of a river, a pattern of waves, or wind action on desert sand. A simple addition of a bird or animal painted on the board will bring the scene to life.

Select boards for the beauty of the woodgrain. Sand lightly, front, edges and corners. A small hobby torch is used to lightly burn the wood and make the grain stand out. The torch is heated by a small can of propane or butane fuel which is inserted at the bottom of the torch nozzle.

With gloved hands, hold the torch about a foot from your board; pass the torch back and forth until the board is burned an even light brown (*Photo 27*).

Use a medium grade of steel wool to rub the board down smooth. Once smooth, the board is ready for painting.

Photo 27. Board is burned with torch to bring out grain of wood.

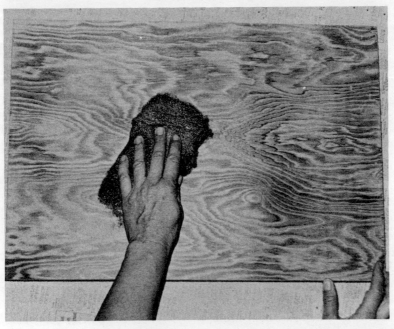

Photo 28. Steel wool rubbing further emphasizes woodgrain.

Keep your patterns simple. Too busy a design will over-shadow the pattern of the woodgrain. Work out your design on tracing paper first. Arrange it on the board and trace with carbon paper. Paint with acrylics, using colors comple-mentary with the golden tones of the wood.

Varnish with two coats of varathene, following direc-tions on the can. This will accentuate the woodgrain. Hang as wall plaques or frame with a narrow molding.

Photo 29. Grain of wood suggests water.

Photo 30. A simple design using woodgrain as sky and water.

Chapter Five

WILDLIFE WOODCUTS

Your own nature designs on woodcuts can be duplicated again and again in notecards or prints for framing. Trace the design on a block of one-inch-thick soft wood (fir or ends of fruit crates are fine for carving).

To avoid having to "think in reverse" as you carve the board, paint entire surface with India ink. Then rub white chalk on the back of the pattern, and trace on. As you carve away the background, the design will appear to you just as it will when printed on paper. All areas that you do not want printed are carved away (*Photo 31*).

You will need a single-edged razor blade or knife, and a carving tool with a U-shaped or a V-shaped gouge. Using knife or razor blade, cut a narrow line around the edge of the design, sloping the cut edge away from the printing surface (you do not want to undercut your design or bits of it may break off in the printing). Next, cut all lines within

Photo 31. Chalk design on India-ink-painted board. Tools needed for carving are shown.

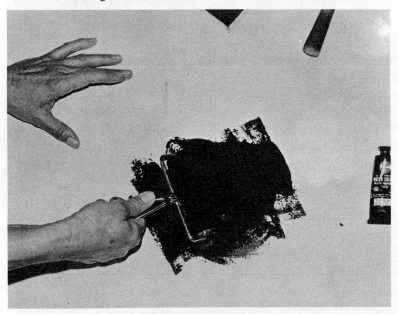

Photo 32. Ink is rolled out on glass slab.

the design. To do this make a cut with the razor blade at an inward angle; turn board around and make a cut from opposite angle, thus removing a thin, V-shaped strip of wood.

Use the gouge tool to remove background around the design. You do not have to carve deeply. Be sure to keep the hand holding the block, away from the cutting tool.

PRINTING

Materials needed for printing are an ink roller (brayer), a pane of heavy glass or a cookie sheet for an inking slab, printing ink which may be either water soluble or of an oil-base (although water soluble ink is easiest to clean up, oil-base inks are the easiest to print with), Japanese rice paper or other soft, absorbent paper for printing.

Place a small amount of ink on the glass slab and roll back and forth with brayer until ink is evenly spread out. Roll inked brayer over the wood block, coating only the raised surface. (*Photo 32*)

Carefully place the printing paper over the inked block. Working from center outward, rub with palm of hand or the back of a wooden spoon (*Photo 33*). Set print aside to dry. Mat and frame print or trim to size and glue on folded card with matching envelope. (*Photo 34*)

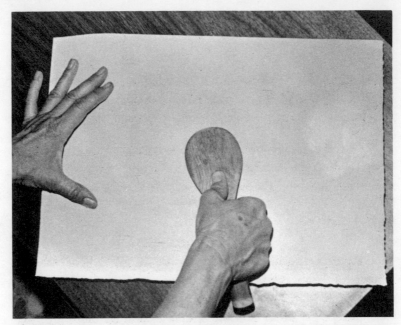

Photo 33. Rice paper placed on inked board is rubbed with wooden spoon.

Photo 34. Wood-cut print.

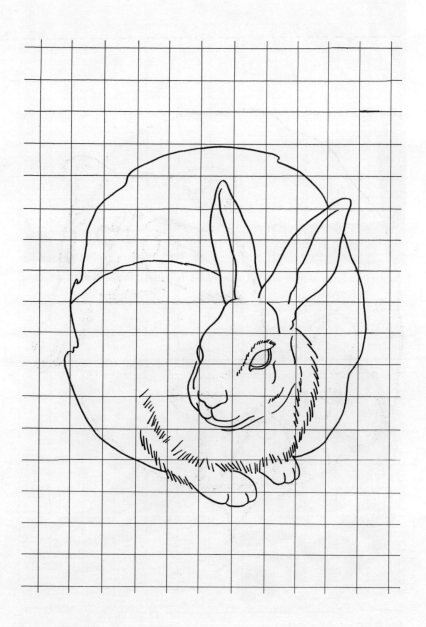

Pattern Chart 1. Varying Hare.

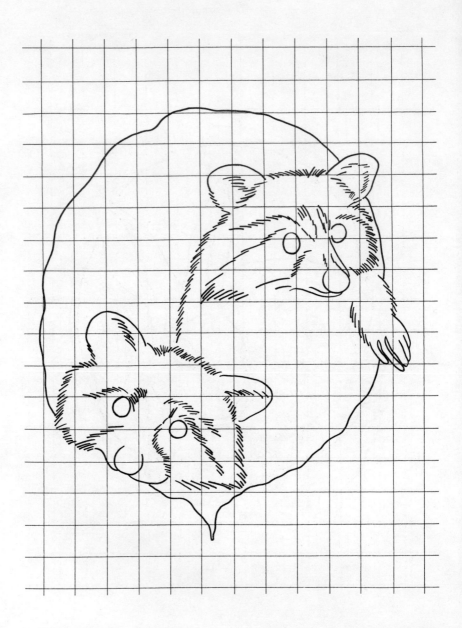

Pattern Chart 2. Raccoons.

(Cut along broken line.)

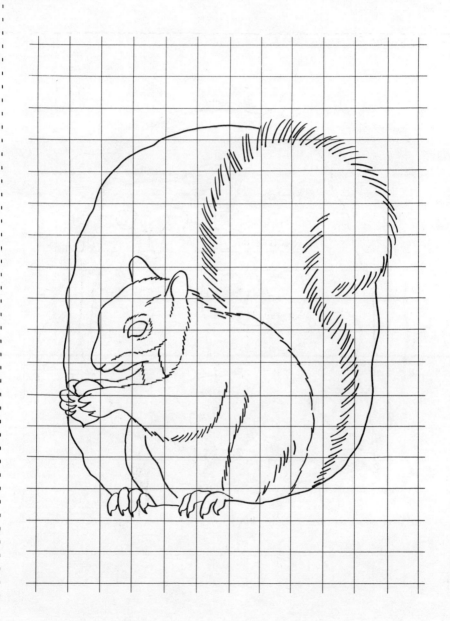

Pattern Chart 3. Gray Squirrel.

Pattern Chart 4. Screech Owls.

(Cut along broken line.)

Pattern Chart 5. Cougar Kitten.

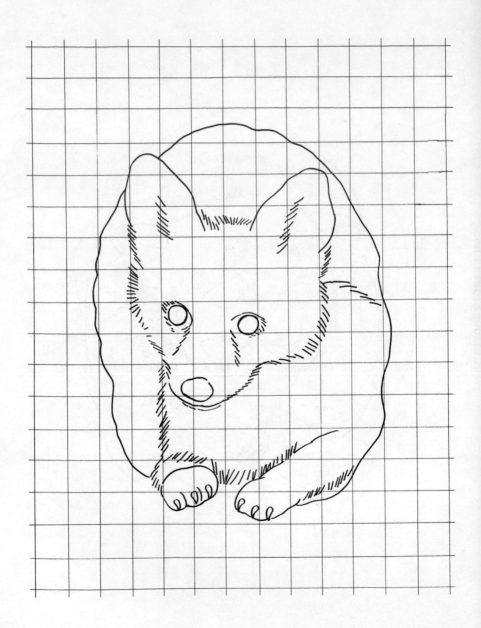

Pattern Chart 6. Red Fox.

(Cut along broken line.)

Pattern Chart 7. Bear Cub.

Pattern Chart 8. Golden-mantled Squirrels.

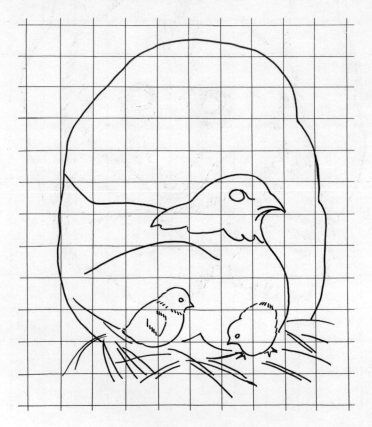

Pattern Chart 9. Ruffed Grouse.